SPIRIT OF

THE BLUEBELL
RAILWAY

MATT ALLEN

First published in Great Britain in 2009

British Library Cataloguing-in-Publication Data
A CIP record for this title is available from the British Library

ISBN 978 1 906887 63 6

PiXZ Books
Halsgrove House, Ryelands Industrial Estate,
Bagley Road, Wellington, Somerset TA21 9PZ
Tel: 01823 653777
Fax: 01823 216796
email: sales@halsgrove.com

An imprint of Halstar Ltd, part of the Halsgrove group of companies
Information on all Halsgrove titles is available at: www.halsgrove.com

Printed and bound by Grafiche Flaminia, Italy

Introduction

The magnificent Bluebell Railway is mainly run by volunteers and operates steam services between Sheffield Park and Kingscote in Sussex. It has over 180,000 visitors per year and is also one of the major Heritage Railways in the UK.

On 1 Aug 1882 the line from Lewes to East Grinstead was opened, primarily intended for freight. There was also a spur that connected Horsted Keynes to Ardingly and Haywards Heath, opened in 1883. The Southern Railway absorbed the whole line in 1923, but by this time the decline had set in. Under nationalisation, British Railways took over in 1948 and by the early 1950s plans for the line's closure were being drawn up. Following representations by a local resident, Miss Madge Bessemer, it was discovered the closure was illegal. However, after a public enquiry held in Lewes in October 1957, the legal constraints were overcome by B.R. and on 16 March 1958 the line closed for a second and final time.

On 24 December 1959, a group of volunteers, keen not to see the line disappear into history, were able to lease the 4½ mile section of line from Sheffield Park to the south of Horsted Keynes under a five year term. The first items of rolling stock began to arrive on 17 May 1960 with the first trains running for the newly formed 'Bluebell Railway Ltd' on 7 August 1960. In 1967 a huge step forward was made when the lease of the line was converted into an outright purchase. The Bluebell Railway always had an eye on extension. Gradually the railway moved north. By 1992 trains were running through West Hoathley tunnel, and 1994 saw the service extended to Kingscote. This is not the end of the story as plans to extend north from Kingscote to East Grinstead are at an advanced stage with the achievement of being reconnected to the national network at East Grinstead on the horizon.

Matt Allen

The Bluebell Railway carries 180,000 visitors per year – vintage trains like this explain why.

With the brazier burning, 34100 'Appledore' sits in the platform at Sheffield Park.

The Bluebell's main engine shed is at Sheffield Park; locomotives can often be seen being prepared for the day's trains.

Locomotives awaiting long-term restoration are also stored undercover at Sheffield Park.

E4 class locomotive number 32473 is seen heading towards
Sheffield Park with a train from Kingscote.

9F locomotive 92240 was built at Crewe in October 1958 and is currently awaiting overhaul.

Schools class locomotive number 928 'Stowe' and T9 class locomotive number 120 are seen in the yard at Sheffield Park.

'Stepney' bathes in lovely light
at the end of a day's work.

A train is seen waiting to depart
Sheffield Park with the 9 mile journey
to Kingscote ahead of it.

32473 passes through Ketches Lane Halt with a southbound demonstration freight train.

21C123 'Blackmore Vale' is seen passing through Ketches Lane Halt
in the opposite direction to the previous photograph.

Standard Tank number 80151 is beginning the climb up Freshfield Bank as it heads from Sheffield Park to Horsted Keynes.

'Pullman' dining trains are extremely popular at the railway,
allowing diners to enjoy a 5 course meal 'steam style'.

Opposite: On a stunning December morning 7F locomotive
number 53809 is seen on a photographers' charter.

753 was a short term visitor to the railway making a fine sight on this mixed train.

Opposite: Freshfield Bank has a gradient of 1-75 which gives
the locomotives a chance to stretch their legs.

Dukedog number 9017 makes an interesting sight with the
Pullman coaches on a frosty (and very cold!) morning.

53809 is seen the head of a 'Santa Special' train.
This locomotive is normally based at the Midland Railway Centre.

Many many hours of restoration are required to create a scene like this.

34059 'Sir Archibald Sinclair' was returned to steam early in 2009 for the first time since 1966.

21C123 is seen approaching 'Broken Bridge'. Of interest is the banana van directly behind the locomotive.

41284 (actually 41312 renumbered) is approaching 'Broken Bridge' at the top of Freshfield Bank.

Opposite: Both 01 class locomotive number 65 and C Class locomotive number 592 (leading) are resplendent in their South East & Chatham Railway livery.

West Country class locomotive 21C123 would have been at home in
South East England during its service with the Southern and British Railways.

A classic Great Western branchline train deep in Southern territory!
1450 and an autocoach are seen heading south toward Sheffield Park.

With a dark sky in the background, 32473 catches the late
evening light during a photographers' special.

Opposite: 80151 at the head of a 'Santa Special' making a great head of steam.

History was made on 7 March 2009 when 73136 worked the first ever diesel-hauled passenger train at the Bluebell Railway.

Bulleid Pacific, 34059 is seen at Monteswood Lane with a northbound train.

Number 672 'Fenchurch' was built in 1872. After finishing its service with
British Railways it was purchased by the Bluebell in 1964.

34007 'Wadebridge' is seen in Lindfield Wood on Remembrance Sunday,
hence the poppies adorning the front of the locomotive.

Lindfield Wood is a great place to see spring flowers,
in this case the railway's namesakes 'bluebells'.

In the same location as the previous photograph 34059 is seen heading a northbound train. This location is about 1 mile south of Horsted Keynes.

Opposite: Holywell is a good location to photograph trains, in this photograph 32473 is seen heading south.

The railway has a fine collection of historic rolling stock. Some of the Pullman coaches seen in this photograph date from the 1920s.

34100 'Appledore' (actually 34028 in disguise) was a visitor to the line from its base at the Swanage Railway.

'Three Arch Bridge' is one of the well known landmarks on the line.
53809 passes under the bridge as it approaches Horsted Keynes Station.

A different angle on Three Arch Bridge as the E4 heads a
demonstration freight train south from Horsted Keynes.

Opposite: U Class locomotive number 1638 catches some
lovely winter light on a photographers' special.

The field adjacent to the line south of Horsted Keynes is a regular haunt for railway photographers. Here 80151 heads a rake of Bulleid coaches.

Opposite: From the opposite side of the line to the previous photograph 53809 is silhouetted on a cold December day.

An authentic
'Metropolitan
Railway' train
with locomotive
Met 1 heading
a rake of teak
coaches.

Ivatt-designed locomotive number 41312 was another
visitor to the line from its base at the Mid Hants Railway.

34100 'Appledore' headed the last ever steam hauled 'Golden Arrow' boat train. This event was recreated for a photographers' special.

32473 is seen taking water in the yard at Horsted Keynes.

Opposite:
7F number 53809 was originally constructed for use on the Somerset and Dorset line, being built at Darlington in 1925.

'Blackmore Vale' heads a Pullman train towards Horsted Keynes.
The coach at the head of the train, 'Christine', was built in 1928.

34028 'Eddystone' is seen at Horsted Keynes Station during a special nightshoot.

'The next train at platform 3 is for Kingscote', meanwhile a freight train is waiting to head north from platform 2.

Horsted Keynes Station is a real gem with some lovely period features.
41312 completes this scene with an authentic branchline train.

A timeless scene outside Horsted Keynes Station.
Nothing indicates this photograph was taken in 2006.

The driver of 32473 relaxes during a break between serivces on a lovely spring day.

Opposite: 1638 departs Horsted Keynes under threatening skies. 1638 was
the 114th engine to leave Barry scrapyard, arriving at the Bluebell in July 1980.

The driver of this Scammell 'Mechanical Horse' dating from 1957 doesn't seem to be observing the signs outside Horsted Keynes Station.

Opposite:
The railway runs a number of 'driver experience' courses where members of the public can pay to drive and fire a steam locomotive, as seen here.

The crews of Bulleid Pacifics 34081 '92 Squadron' and
34007 'Wadebridge' catch up with the day's gossip.

Terrier number 8 'Freshwater' visited the line from the Isle of Wight Steam Railway for a special event held at the Bluebell.

One of the regular special occasions held is a 'War on the Line' event, when the railway is transported back to the 1940s as are its visitors.

'Blackmore Vale' is beginning its journey from Horsted Keynes to Kingscote on a lovely summer's day, seen passing under Leamland Bridge.

'Stepney' takes a break at Horsted Keynes.

Sharpthorne Tunnel featured in the 1999 version of the classic story 'The Railway Children'. 32473 is seen exiting the southern end of the tunnel.

1450 and its autocoach are caught heading south from Kingscote.

Kingscote is the current northern terminus of the line, although an extension to East Grinstead is planned in the near future.

672 'Fenchurch' is starting the 9 mile journey south to Sheffield Park. The driver is ready to exchange the signal token.

In driving rain the 'U Boat' number 1638 pulls into Kingscote Station with a reconstruction of a 'Southern Railway' freight train.

The Bluebell Railway is one of the premier tourist attractions in the south, a great way to be transported back to they heyday of steam travel.